Developing Reading Skills Using Fairy Tales

Grades 1-3

Written by Ruth Solski
Illustrated by Jimmy Claridy and S&S Learning Materials

About the author:
Ruth Solski was an educator for 30 years. She has written many educational resources over the years and is the founder of S&S Learning Materials. As a writer, her main goal is to provide teachers with a useful tool they can implement in their classrooms to bring the joy of learning to children.

ISBN 978-1-55035-920-6
Copyright 2008

Published in the U.S.A by:
On The Mark Press
3909 Witmer Road PMB 175
Niagara Falls, New York
14305
www.onthemarkpress.com

Published in Canada by:
S&S Learning Materials
15 Dairy Avenue
Napanee, Ontario
K7R 1M4
www.sslearning.com

Permission to Reproduce

Permission is granted to the individual teacher who purchases one copy of this book to reproduce the student activity material for use in his/her classroom only. Reproduction of these materials for an entire school or for a school system, or for other colleagues or for commercial sale is **strictly prohibited**. No part of this publication may be transmitted in any form or by any means, electronic, mechanical, recording or otherwise without the prior written permission of the publisher. "We acknowledge the financial support of the Government of Canada through the Book Publishing Industry Development Program (BPIDP) for this project." Printed in Canada. All Rights Reserved

At A Glance

Learning Expectations	Goldilocks and the Three Bears	The Three Little Pigs	Little Red Riding Hood	Three Billy Goats Gruff	Little Red Hen	The Gingerbread Man	The Ugly Duckling	The Elves and the Shoemaker	The Four Musicians	Jack and the Beanstalk
Reading Comprehension Skills										
Recalling Details	•		•		•	•		•	•	
Recalling Events				•	•			•	•	
Sequential Ordering of Story Events		•				•	•			
Drawing Conclusions	•									
Character Evaluation			•	•		•				•
Making Inferences	•		•	•	•	•		•	•	
Phonetic Skills										
Initial Consonants	•					•				
Long and Short Vowels		•	•		•		•			•
Sound Substitution		•		•	•					•
Blend Recognition				•						
Digraph Recognition								•		
Rhyming Words				•					•	
Vocabulary Skills										
Antonyms, Synonyms	•			•						•
Word Families		•			•					
Adding Suffixes			•							
Syllabication, Compound Words						•				•
Alphabetical Order				•						
Word Meanings							•	•	•	
Creative Thinking										
Dramatization	•	•								
Brainstorming Ideas			•		•				•	
Illustrating Ideas			•		•	•	•		•	•
Developing Story Writing Skills				•		•		•		•

Developing Reading Skills Using Fairy Tales

Table of Contents

At A Glance™		2
Teacher Assessment Rubric		4
Student Assessment Rubric		5
About This Book		6
Fairy Tale 1:	**Goldilocks and the Three Bears**	10
	Reading Activities	14
Fairy Tale 2:	**The Three Little Pigs**	18
	Reading Activities	22
Fairy Tale 3:	**Little Red Riding Hood**	26
	Reading Activities	29
Fairy Tale 4:	**The Three Billy Goats Gruff**	33
	Reading Activities	37
Fairy Tale 5:	**The Little Red Hen**	41
	Reading Activities	45
Fairy Tale 6:	**The Gingerbread Man**	49
	Reading Activities	53
Fairy Tale 7:	**The Ugly Duckling**	58
	Reading Activities	62
Fairy Tale 8:	**The Elves and the Shoemaker**	66
	Reading Activities	70
Fairy Tale 9:	**The Four Musicians**	74
	Reading Activities	78
Fairy Tale 10:	**Jack and the Beanstalk**	82
	Reading Activities	86
Fairy Tale Creative Activity Cards		90
Answer Key		93
Manipulative Sequence Activities		97

Teacher Assessment Rubric

Student's Name: _____ **Date:** _____

Criteria	Level 1	Level 2	Level 3	Level 4
Reading Comprehension Skills				
Able to recall story facts and events	Limited	Some	Often	Well
Able to evaluate the personality of characters	Limited	Some	Often	Well
Able to form opinions and make inferences about characters and events	Limited	Some	Often	Well
Able to put story events in order	Limited	Some	Often	Well
Phonetic Concepts and Skills				
Recognition and application of initial consonants	Limited	Some	Often	Well
Recognition and application of long and short vowels	Limited	Some	Often	Well
Recognition and application of blends and digraphs	Limited	Some	Often	Well
Identification of rhyming words	Limited	Some	Often	Well
Vocabulary Skills				
Identification of antonyms, synonyms, and compound words	Limited	Some	Often	Well
Ability to arrange words in alphabetical order	Limited	Some	Often	Well
Recognition of syllabication	Limited	Some	Often	Well
Creative Thinking				
Participation in dramatic activities	Limited	Some	Often	Well
Ability to brainstorm and illustrate ideas	Limited	Some	Often	Well
Ability to express ideas in complete sentences	Limited	Some	Often	Well
Ability to express ideas to form a story or a description	Limited	Some	Often	Well

Student Self-Assessment Rubric

Name: _____ Date: _____

Put a check mark ✓ in each box that best tells how you worked. Then add your points to get your score.

Expectations	The Way I Worked			
	Always (4 points)	Most of the Time (3 points)	Sometimes (2 points)	A Little (1 point)
✓ I listen well in class during lessons.				
✓ I listen well when the teacher talks about the work.				
✓ I do my work neatly and carefully.				
✓ I can read the fairy tales by myself.				
✓ I can read the activities without help.				
✓ I join in when everyone reads the story out loud.				
✓ I know how to make my work better.				
✓ I know the areas I need to improve.				

1. I liked _____

_____

2. I learned _____

_____

3. I want to read _____

_____

My Score: _____

Developing Reading Skills Using Fairy Tales

Introduction

Developing Reading Skills Using Fairy Tales is a resource book that contains ten popular fairy tales that have been retold and are accompanied by practice work sheets for a variety of reading skills.

The ten stories vary in reading difficulty from first grade to the end of grade three to meet a range of needs. At the top of each page the skill or skills to be practiced are indicated for teacher usage.

Each story is followed by four reproducible pages of activities that focus on the development and reinforcement of four different areas of reading. They are reading comprehension, phonics, vocabulary development, and creative thinking.

Ways to Implement the Stories

A. Teacher-Directed Lessons with:
    - small groups of children all reading at the same level
    - an individual student
    - the entire class to support a theme or a unit being studied

B. Each story may be used as:
    - an instructional tool or device to teach and reinforce reading skills
    - partner reading to develop fluency and the development of independent reading

C. Check each story for any vocabulary that the students may find difficult to understand or decode. Introduce this vocabulary to your students on a chart or the chalkboard.

D. The stories may be reproduced and mounted on letter size file folders for independent usage.

Example: **Front of Folder**   **Inside Folder**   **Back of Folder**

 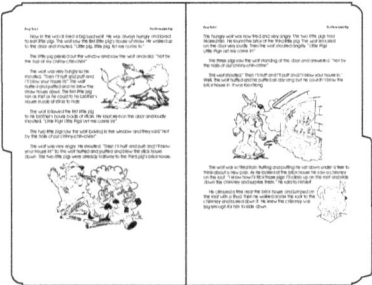 

These stories could be placed at a Fairy Tale Center for students to read independently or with a reading partner.

Ways to Implement Skill Activity Pages

A. Skill Areas:

Each story has four skill oriented activity pages. These pages focus on reading comprehension, phonics, vocabulary development, and creative thinking.

B. Activity Page Implementation:

1. The pages may be reproduced and used to teach or to practice necessary skills students require.

2. The pages of the story and the skill pages may be reproduced and then collated as a set for a group or the entire class to read and complete independently by the students.

3. The pages of the story and the follow-up activities may be used to make transparencies to be used for classroom instruction, to review previously learned skills, and large group reading.

4. Review written directions for student understanding so they understand fully how to complete the assignment independently.

Thematic Reading Approach to Fairy Tales

If you wish to implement fairy tale reading as a theme in your classroom use some of the following suggestions to present this reading genre to your class.

1. Introduce the fairy tale theme with one that is on a DVD or read one that is popular with your class.

2. Discuss the story line, the characters, and the values expressed in it.

3. Brainstorm with your students various fairy tales that they know and list the titles on a chart.

4. As the students proceed during the theme discuss the various aspects of fairy tales such as the characters, the magical objects used, and the magical happenings that take place.

5. Share a different fairy tale each day with your class for enjoyment and to develop good listening skills.

6. Discuss the following concepts found in fairy tales:

    - values and morals in the story such as good over evil, destruction of property, holding someone hostage, breaking and entering, stealing, lying, honesty, deception, etc. (adjust according to the level of understanding of your students)

    - ways fairy tales are similar such as good prevails over evil, most have a happy ending, evil characters, good characters, usually has a moral or a value, magical events take place in many, etc.

- characteristics of characters such as evil, good, innocent, poor, rich, royalty, wealthy, animals that are humanized, deceitful, tricky, sly, dishonest, vengeful, mean, cunning, sneaky, kind, princesses, princes, kings, queens

- magical elements in fairy tales such as wands, apples, spells, potions, changing shape, fairy godmothers, giants, ogres, dragons, fairies, elves, dwarfs, secret passageways, magic beans, a harp that sings, a hen that lays golden eggs, magical shoes, a magic carpet, a magic lamp, a magical mirror

7. At a listening center in your classroom have your students take turns listening to a fairy tale while following the text in a book.

8. Establish a drama center in your classroom. At the center provide a variety of props and costumes such as a witch's hat, crown, golden ball, wolf ears headband, pig ears headband, bear masks, wand, night cap, night gown, a princess dress, red cape with a hood, basket, bag of golden coins, goat masks, etc. Small groups of students could choose a fairy tale and dramatize it.

9. Listen to music that has been written for movies about fairy tales such as Cinderella, Snow White, Aladdin and his Wonderful Lamp, and Jack and the Beanstalk.

10. Teach your class songs that have been written for fairy tale movies.

11. End your reading theme with a "Fairy Tale Day". Encourage your students to dress as their favorite fairy tale character for the day. Parade around the school to show them off.

12. Plan an excursion to a local theater to watch a performance of a fairy tale or invite a touring company to the school.

Colored Manipulative Sequence Activities

At the end of this book there are 10 colored pages containing activities for the development of sequential ordering for five fairy tales. The stories are Goldilocks and the Three Bears, The Three Little Pigs, Little Red Riding Hood, The Elves and the Shoemaker, and Jack and the Beanstalk.

Story Sequence Picture Cards

The story sequence pictures are to be cut out, mounted on a sturdy backing, and laminated to insure longer usage. Store the sequence picture cards in an envelope labeled with the title of the fairy tale and the instructions on how to use them.

Story Sequence Sentence Strips

The fairy tale sentence strips are to be cut out and mounted on a sturdy backing and laminated to ensure longer usage. Store the sentence strips in an envelope labeled with the title of the fairy tale and the instructions on how to use them.

Story Sequence Pictures and Story Sentence Strips

The story picture sequence cards and the story sentence strips could be stored in the same envelope. The student will match the story pictures and story sentence strips and then arrange them in the correct sequential ordering of the fairy tale.

Felt Board Sequence Activity Cards

The story picture sequence cards and the story sequence sentence strips could also have felt glued to the back in order to be used on a felt board to tell the sequential development orally of each story. The story picture sequence cards and the story sequence sentence strips could also be used as a matching activity involving reading the text and then matching it to the correct picture. Once the sentences and pictures are matched the story could then be arranged in the correct sequential order.

Fairy Tale Books

The story sequence pictures could be photocopied for student usage to produce their own storybooks. The pictures are to be glued in the book in the correct sequential order. Under each picture the students can write a short description of the event.

Example:

The sequence sentence strips could also be photocopied for student usage. The sentence strips could be cut out and glued in the correct sequential order in a story booklet. The students are to illustrate their own pictures to match the sentences.

Fairy Tale 1

Goldilocks and the Three Bears

Once upon a time there were three bears. There was a Papa Bear, a Mama Bear, and a Baby Bear. They lived in a house in the woods.

Every morning Mama Bear made some porridge. She put the porridge in three bowls to cool. The porridge was too hot to eat so the three bears went for a walk.

One day, a little girl named Goldilocks was playing in the woods. She found a pretty little house. Goldilocks wanted to know who lived there so she knocked on the door. No one came to the door, so Goldilocks went inside.

Goldilocks saw three bowls of porridge on the table in the kitchen. She was hungry. Goldilocks picked up a spoon and tasted the porridge from the biggest bowl. It was too hot! So she tried the porridge in the middle-size bowl. It was too cold! Then she tried the porridge in the small bowl. It was just right so she ate it all up.

Goldilocks looked around the house and found three chairs near the fireplace. First she sat in the great big chair. She found it way too hard.

Next she sat in the middle-size chair. Goldilocks found this chair way too soft.

Then she sat in the smallest chair and it felt just right .... until it broke with a loud **SNAP**!

Goldilocks saw a set of stairs. She climbed the stairs and found a big bedroom with three beds. Goldilocks was tired and wanted to rest.

First she climbed onto the great big bed. It was too bumpy and hard to sleep on.

Next she tried the middle-sized bed. It was too soft and fluffy to sleep on.

Then Goldilocks tried the little bed. She climbed on it to rest and found it just right. It was not too hard and not too soft. Soon she was fast asleep on the little bed.

Before long, the three bears returned home. They were very hungry and went straight to the kitchen to eat their porridge.

Papa Bear picked up his spoon and looked at his porridge. "Hmmmm" growled Papa Bear. "It looks like someone has been eating my porridge."

Mama Bear looked at her bowl of porridge and cried, "Someone has been eating my porridge, too. Some of my porridge is missing from my bowl."

Then Baby Bear looked at his bowl of porridge and cried loudly, "Someone has been eating my porridge and it's all gone!" Big tears fell down his face.

The three bears knew that someone had been in their house. Next the three bears went into the living room and looked at their chairs by the fireplace.

"Someone has been sitting in my chair!" growled Papa Bear.

"Someone has been sitting in my chair, too!" said Mama Bear excitedly.

Then Baby Bear saw his chair and cried out loudly, "Someone has been sitting in my chair and has broken it!"

The three bears went upstairs to their bedroom. They looked all around the room.

Papa Bear roared, **"Someone has been on my bed as the pillows are all messy!"**

Mama Bear excaimed in surprise, **"Someone has been on my bed as my covers are all over the place!"**

Then Baby Bear saw Goldilocks. He shouted, **"Someone is sleeping on my bed!"**

When Goldilocks heard Baby Bear's squeaky voice she woke up. Looking down at her were three bears. Goldilocks was so surprised and scared that she jumped off the bed and ran out of the bears' house and all the way home.

The three bears were never visited by Goldilocks again.

Fairy Tale 1: Reading Comprehension - Recalling Details, Making Inferences

Goldilocks and the Three Bears

Answer each question with a good sentence.

1. Who were the characters in the story?
   _____
   _____
   _____

2. Why did the three bears go out for a walk?
   _____
   _____

3. Draw pictures of the three different things that Goldilocks found in the three bear's house. Name each one.

4. Why did Goldilocks like the Baby Bear's bowl, chair, and bed the best?
   _____
   _____

5. Do you think Goldilocks should have gone into the bears' house when they were not home? Tell why.
   _____
   _____

6. What do you think the bears might do to their home after Goldilocks' visit?
   _____
   _____

Goldilocks and the Three Bears

Mother Bear put porridge in three bowls.

Bowl begins with the sound that "Bb" makes.

Cut out the pictures that begin with the sound that "Bb" makes.

Glue them in the big bowl.

Bb bowl

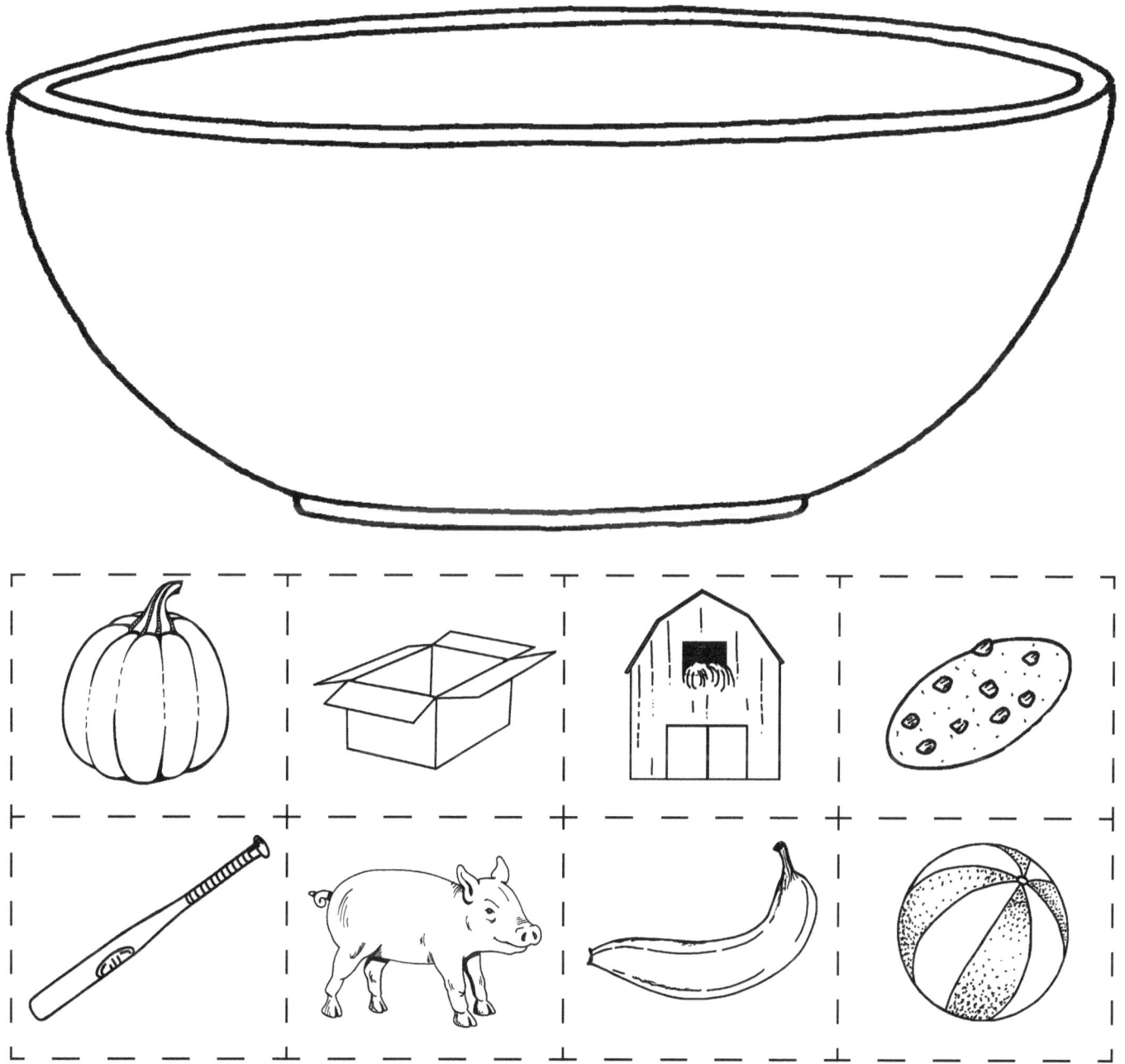

Fairy Tale 1: Word Study - Antonyms, Synonyms

Goldilocks and the Three Bears

A. Choose words from the bowl to make pairs of antonyms.

1. hard _____

2. big _____

3. cool _____

4. first _____

5. off _____

6. awake _____

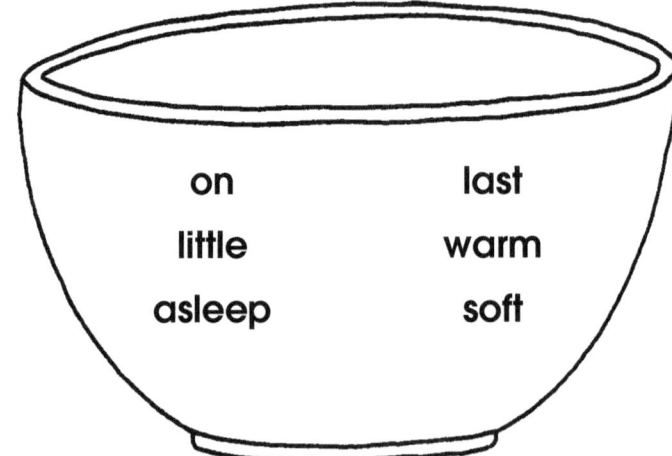

on   last
little   warm
asleep   soft

B. Match the words in the bowl to words that mean the same.

1. knock _____

2. little _____

3. shouted _____

4. bowls _____

5. tasted _____

6. biggest _____

7. rest _____

8. woods _____

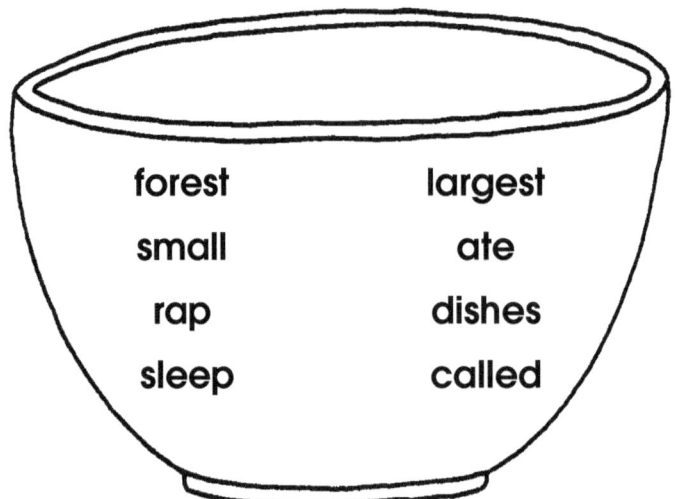

forest   largest
small   ate
rap   dishes
sleep   called

Fairy Tale 1: Creative Thinking - Retelling a Story

Goldilocks and the Three Bears

Color the pictures in the shapes neatly.

Cut along the dotted lines carefully.

Tape each fairy tale character to one end of a ruler.

Now you have a fairy tale stick puppet.

Use the stick puppets to tell the story of Goldilocks and the three Bears.

Fairy Tale 2

The Three Little Pigs

Once upon a time there were three little pigs. They lived with their mother in a little house. One day, the three pigs told their mother that it was time for them to go out in the world on their own. The three pigs kissed their mother good-bye and set off down the road.

Soon they met a man with a wagon of straw. The first little pig wanted some of the straw to build his house. "Please, sir, may I have some of your straw for my house?" asked the first little pig. The man gave the pig some of his straw and then went on his way. The first little pig said good-bye to his brothers and went off to build his house of straw.

Off went the two little pigs down the road. Soon they met a man with a cart full of sticks. The second little pig wanted some of the sticks to build a house. "Please, sir, may I have some of the sticks on your cart?" The man gave the pig some of the sticks and went on his way.
The second little pig said good-bye to his brother and went off to build his house of sticks.

The third little pig waved good-bye to his brother and walked down the road. Along came a man with a load of bricks on his cart. The little pig stopped the man and asked, "Please, sir may I have some of your bricks? The man gave him some bricks and went on his way. The third little pig used the bricks to build a strong house.

Now in the woods lived a big bad wolf. He was always hungry and loved to eat little pigs. The wolf saw the first little pig's house of straw. He walked up to the door and shouted, **"Little pig! Little pig! Let me come in!"**

The little pig peeked out the window and saw the wolf and said, "Not by the hair of my chinny-chin-chin!"

The wolf was very hungry so he shouted, **"Then I'll huff and I'll puff and I'll blow your house in!"** The wolf huffed and puffed and he blew the straw house down. The first little pig ran as fast as he could to his brother's house made of sticks to hide.

The wolf followed the first little pig to his brother's house made of sticks. He knocked on the door and loudly shouted, **"Little Pigs! Little Pigs! Let me come in!"**

The two little pigs saw the wolf looking in the window and they said, "Not by the hairs of our chinny-chin-chins!"

The wolf was very angry. He shouted, **"Then I'll huff and I'll puff and I'll blow your house in!"** While the wolf huffed and puffed and blew the stick house down, the two little pigs were already halfway to the third pig's brick house.

The hungry wolf was now tired and very angry. The two little pigs had tricked him. He found the brick house of the third little pig. The wolf knocked on the door very loudly. Then the wolf shouted angrily, **"Little Pigs! Little Pigs! Let me come in!"**

The three pigs saw the wolf standing at the door and answered, "Not by the hairs of our chinny-chin-chins!"

The wolf shouted, **"Then I'll huff and I'll puff and I'll blow your house in!"** Well, the wolf huffed and he puffed all day long but he couldn't blow the brick house in. It was too strong!

The wolf was so tired from huffing and puffing he sat down under a tree to think about a new plan. As he looked at the brick house, he saw a chimney on the roof. "I know how I'll trick those pigs! I'll climb up on the roof and slide down the chimney and surprise them," he said to himself.

He climbed a tree near the brick house and jumped on the roof with a thud. Then he walked across the roof to the chimney and looked down it. He knew the chimney was big enough for him to slide down.

Now the Little pigs heard the thud and knew that it was the wolf. In the fireplace hung a pot of water. Quickly the pigs put more wood on the fire to make the water get very hot. "Now we have a surprise for the big, bad wolf!" said the three little pigs happily.

Suddenly the wolf shouted down the chimney, **"Little Pigs, this time you will not get away. I am coming down the chimney to eat you!"** Into the chimney hopped the wolf. He slid down the chimney with a big whoosh and ended with a splash into the pot of boiling water!"

The third little pig quickly put a lid on the pot. That was the end of the big bad wolf. The three little pigs were so happy that they had no one to be afraid of any more. They began to dance about and sing this little song:

**"The big bad wolf has gone away
Gone away, gone away.
Now we can go out to play
In the sunshine every day."**

The three little pigs lived happily in the brick house for many years.

Fairy Tale 2: Reading Comprehension - Sequential Ordering

The Three Little Pigs

Cut and paste the sentences in order to tell the story.

1.	5.
2.	6.
3.	7.
4.	8.

- The wolf blew in the stick house.
- The first pig built a straw house.
- The brick house was too strong for the wolf.
- The wolf blew in the straw house.
- The stick house was built by the second pig.
- The wolf slid down the chimney into a pot of hot water.
- The three little pigs left home.
- The third pig built a brick house.

The Three Little Pigs

The short "i" sound is heard in the word pig.

Look in the story for short "i" words to finish the following sentences about the three little pigs and the big bad wolf.

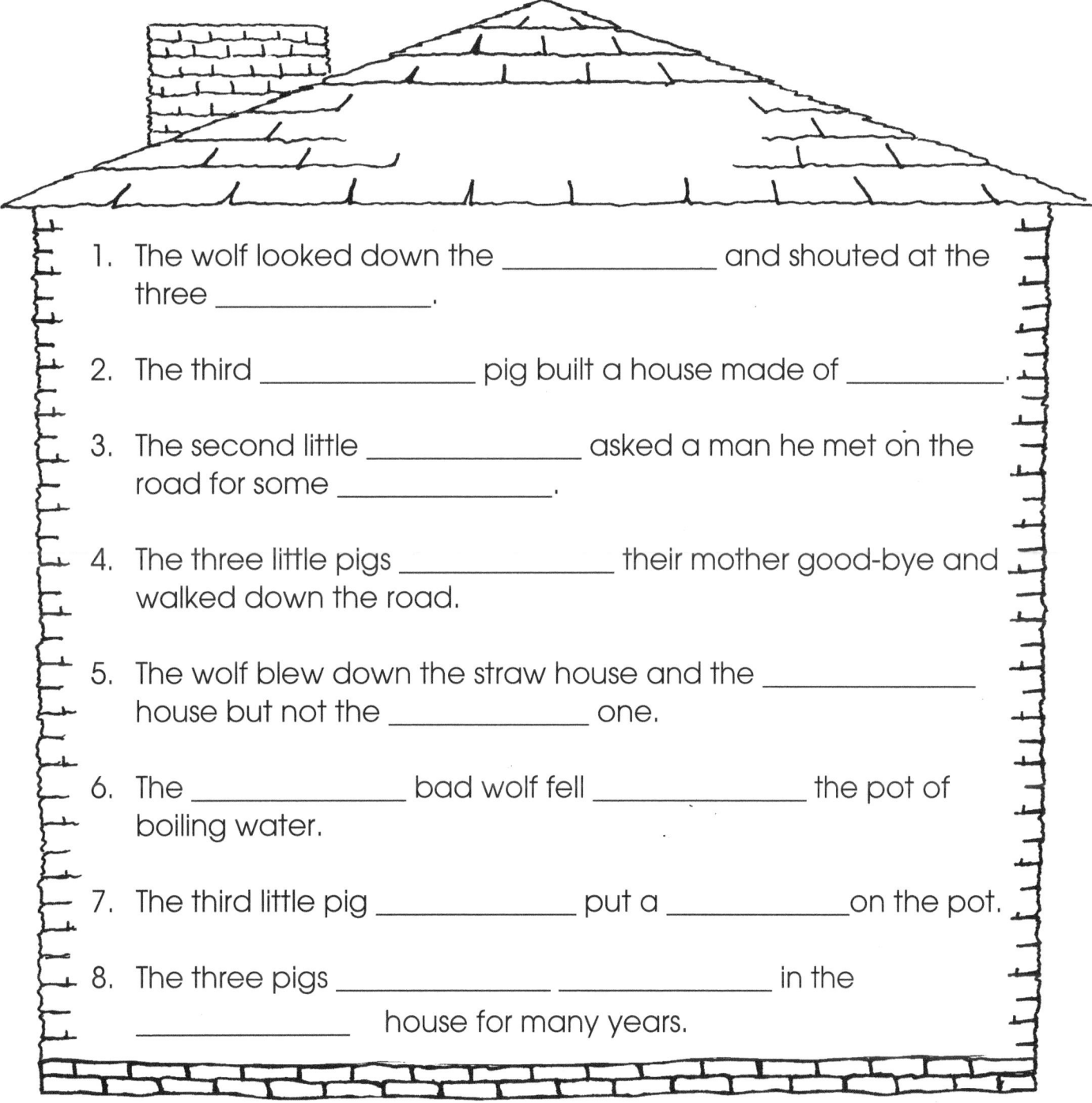

1. The wolf looked down the _____ and shouted at the three _____.

2. The third _____ pig built a house made of _____.

3. The second little _____ asked a man he met on the road for some _____.

4. The three little pigs _____ their mother good-bye and walked down the road.

5. The wolf blew down the straw house and the _____ house but not the _____ one.

6. The _____ bad wolf fell _____ the pot of boiling water.

7. The third little pig _____ put a _____ on the pot.

8. The three pigs _____ _____ in the _____ house for many years.

Fairy Tale 2: Word Study - Word Family "ick"

The Three Little Pigs

Working with the "ick" Word Family

Make new words using "ick".

1. br + ick = _____	5. st + ick = _____
2. ch + ick = _____	6. p + ick = _____
3. th + ick = _____	7. s + ick = _____
4. tr + ick = _____	8. k + ick = _____

Use the words that you made to complete these sentences.

1. The baby _____ hid under its mother.

2. The walls of the brick house were very _____.

3. The little boy felt _____ at school.

4. The pigs played a big _____ on the big bad wolf.

5. The third pig built a strong house made of _____.

6. How far can you _____ the big ball?

7. I will _____ the biggest apple to eat for lunch.

8. The pig hit the wolf with a big _____.

The Three Little Pigs

Color each picture neatly.

Cut along the dotted lines carefully.

Tape each fairy tale character to one end of a ruler.

Now you have a stick puppet.

Use the puppets to put on a play about the story of the Three Little Pigs.

Fairy Tale 3

Little Red Riding Hood

In a house near a woods lived a little girl. She was called Little Red Riding Hood because she wore a red cape with a red hood. One day her mother asked her to take a basket of goodies to her sick Grandmother who lived on the other side of the woods. Her mother told her not to stop or go off the path in the forest. She also told her not to talk to strangers along the way.

Little Red Riding Hood put on her cape, picked up the basket, and skipped happily along the path. She soon forgot her mother's warnings. Red Riding Hood went off the path to pick some flowers for her Grandmother and to listen to the birds sing. There she met a big wolf hiding behind a tree.

"Where are you going little girl?" asked the wolf. "What do you have in your basket?"

"I'm going to visit my Grandmother who lives on the other side of the woods," answered Red Riding Hood. "She is sick and I am taking her some goodies. I must go now as I am not to talk to strangers."

The wolf smiled and said, "Your mother is right. You must hurry on your way to your Grandmother's house." Away went Red Riding Hood skipping down the path. The wolf knew of a shorter way to Grandmother's house and was soon knocking on her door.

"Who is there?" called Grandmother from her bed.

"It is I, Red Riding Hood. I have brought you a basket of goodies," said the wolf in a high, sweet voice.

Grandmother got out of bed and went to answer the door. She opened the door and saw the wolf. Grandmother began to run away, but the wolf grabbed her and put her in a closet and locked the door. He put on one of Grandmother's nightgowns and one of her night caps and climbed into her bed.

The wolf did not have to wait very long. Soon he heard the front door open. Red Riding Hood came into her Grandmother's bedroom.

"Hello, my dear," said the wolf in a high sweet voice. "Please come closer to me, so I can hear and see you better."

Little Red Riding Hood walked closer to her bed. Her Grandmother did not look the same. She saw the wolf's big eyes looking at her.

"Why, Grandmother, what big eyes you have," said Little Red Riding Hood.

The wolf answered in a high sweet voice, "All the better to see you with, my dear!"

Then Red Riding Hood saw the wolf's big ears peeking out of the night cap. "Oh, Grandmother, what big ears you have!" said Red Riding Hood.

"All the better to hear you with, my dear!" said the wolf softly.

Then Red Riding Hood saw the wolf's big teeth and said, "Oh, Grandmother! What big teeth you have!"

"**ALL THE BETTER TO EAT YOU WITH**!" shouted the wolf in his big voice. Then the wolf jumped out of the bed and tried to grab Red Riding Hood.

Red Riding Hood screamed loudly, "**Help! Help**!"

A woodcutter working in the woods heard her screams. He ran to Grandmother's house and waved his ax at the wolf. The wolf was so afraid that he ran out of the house and through the woods and was never seen again. The woodcutter saved Red Riding Hood and unlocked the closet to let her Grandmother out.

Grandmother, Red Riding Hood, and the woodcutter sat down to have a snack of milk and cookies. Red Riding Hood never went off the path to Grandmother's house again.

Fairy Tale 3: Reading Comprehension - Recalling Details

Little Red Riding Hood

Answer each question with a good sentence.

1. What two things will Red Riding Hood do the next time she goes to Grandmother's house?
   _____
   _____

2. Why did Red Riding Hood forget her mother's warnings?
   _____
   _____

3. Why did the wolf get to Grandmother's house first?
   _____
   _____

4. In what three ways did Grandmother not look the same to Red Riding Hood?
   _____
   _____
   _____

5. Who was the villain in the story? Tell why.
   _____
   _____
   _____

6. Who was the hero in the story? Tell why.
   _____
   _____
   _____

Fairy Tale 3: Phonics - Long and Short "a" Vowel Sound

Little Red Riding Hood

Little Red Riding Hood wore a cape and carried a basket of goodies.

The word cape has the long "a" sound and the word basket has the short "a" sound.

On the cape, print the long "a" words and on the basket print the short "a" words.

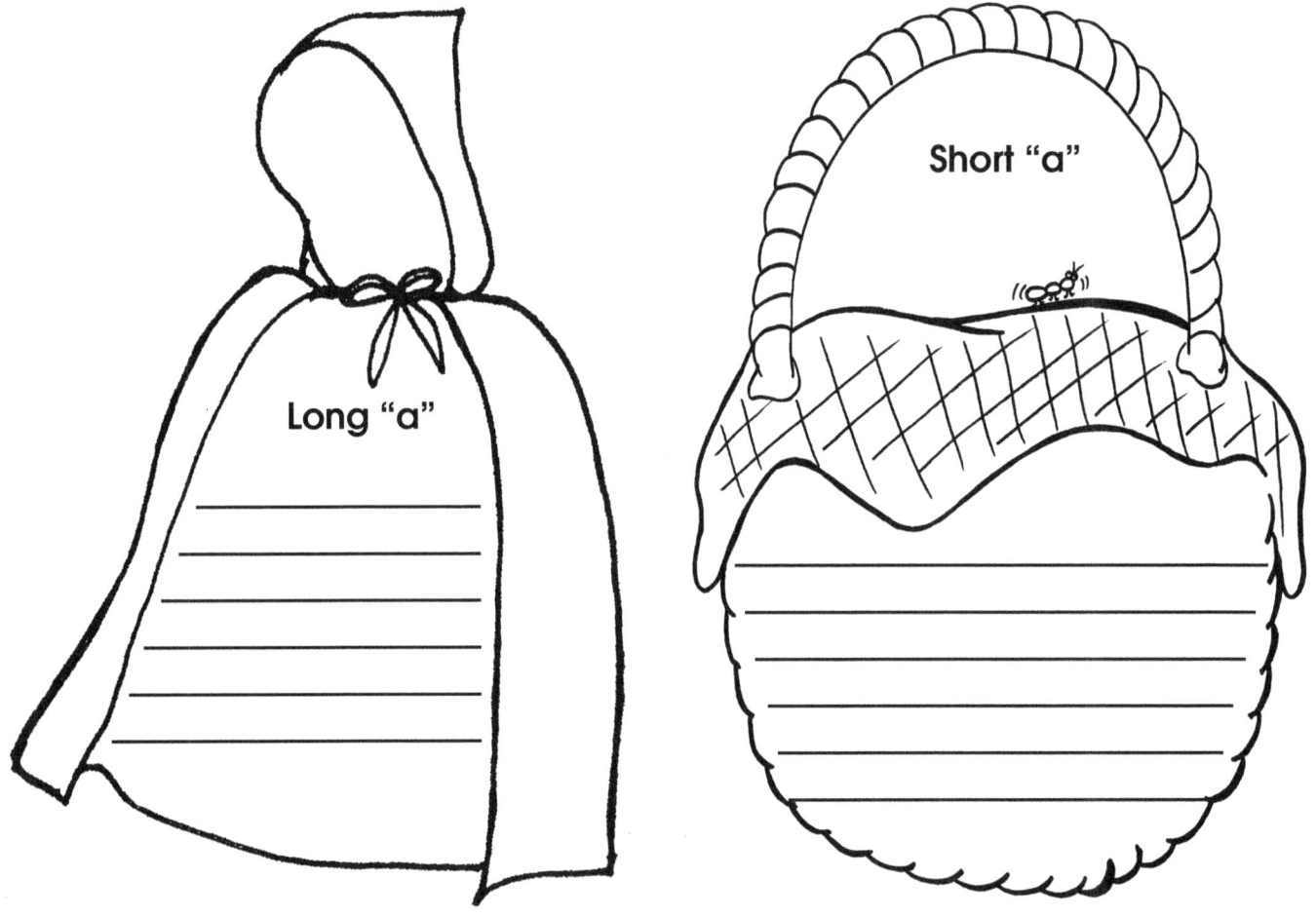

Word Box

strangers	ran	same	day
way	path	saved	caps
grabbed	began	taking	snack

Fairy Tale 3: Word Study: Adding Suffixes

Little Red Riding Hood

Adding Endings

A. Add the endings to the words.

    (ed)   (ing)

1. pick _____ _____
2. jump _____ _____
3. knock _____ _____
4. open _____ _____

B. Add the final letter and the endings.

    (ed)   (ing)

1. stop _____ _____
2. skip _____ _____
3. grab _____ _____

C. Drop the final "e" and add the endings.

    (ed)   (ing)

1. live   _____ _____
2. wave   _____ _____
3. smile _____ _____

D. Complete each sentence with the missing word.

1. Red Riding Hood _____ some flowers in the woods.
2. Grandmother _____ on the other side of the woods
3. The wolf saw the little girl _____ along the path.
4. The wolf _____ on the door of Grandmother's house.

Little Red Riding Hood

Red Riding Hood carried the cookies in a basket.

How do we carry other things?

Draw pictures of ways we carry things from place to place in the boxes.

Print a sentence about each way on the lines beside each box.

1.

2.

3.

The Three Billy Goats Gruff

Once upon a time there lived three billy goats. Their names were Little Billy Goat Gruff, Middle Billy Goat Gruff, and Big Billy Goat Gruff. They lived on the side of a mountain. Every day they ate the grass that grew there.

From the side of the mountain they could see a river with a beautiful meadow on the other side. The meadow was full of beautiful flowers and thick green grass. The grass on their mountain was getting thin and hard to find. The billy goats wanted to go to the meadow on the other side of the river, but they had to go over a stone bridge. Under the bridge lived a mean old troll who loved to eat billy goats.

This troll was grumpy and ugly looking. His eyes were as big as saucers and his nose was long and pointed. Long sharp teeth hung out of his mouth. His hair was straggly and dirty. When he was angry, he whipped about his long scaly tail. No wonder the goats were afraid!

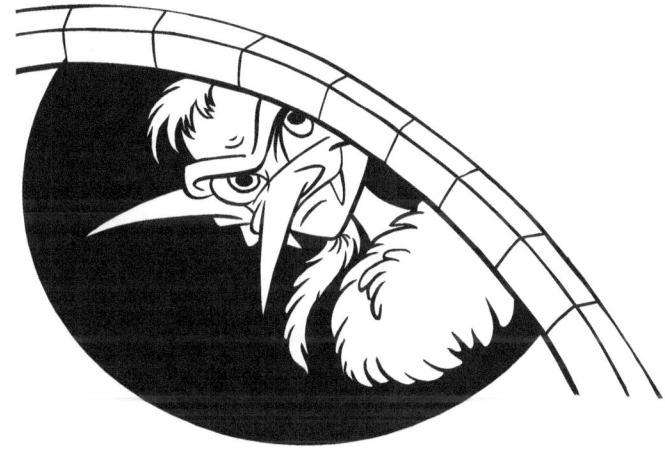

One sunny day, the three billy goats ran out of grass to eat. They decided to go across the bridge to the meadow where the grass grew green and sweet.

Little Billy Goat Gruff went first. He came to the bridge and began to walk across it. Trip, trap! Trip, trap! went his little hoofs softly on the bridge.

"WHO'S THAT TRIP-TRAPPING OVER MY BRIDGE?" called the grumpy old troll.

"It is I," whispered Little Billy Goat Gruff in a wee little voice. "I am going to the meadow to eat the good green grass so I can make myself fat."

"**OH, NO YOU ARE NOT**!" shouted the troll. "**I AM GOING TO GOBBLE YOU UP FOR LUNCH**!"

Oh, please, Mr. Troll! Don't eat me!" begged the Little Billy Goat Gruff. "I'm much too small. Wait for my brother, Middle Billy Goat Gruff. He is much bigger than I am!"

The troll thought for a second. Then he said, "**ALL RIGHT! BE OFF WITH YOU**!"

A little while later Middle Billy Goat Gruff started to trip-trap over the troll's bridge. Trip-trap! Trip-trap! went his feet quickly over the bridge.

"**WHO'S THAT TRIP-TRAPPING ACROSS MY BRIDGE?**" shouted the ugly old troll.

"It is I," answered Middle Billy Goat Gruff in a middle-sized voice. "I am going to the meadow to eat the good green grass so I can get fat."

"**OH, NO YOU ARE NOT**!" shouted the ugly old troll. "**I AM COMING UP THERE TO GOBBLE YOU UP**!"

"No. No. Mr. Troll! Don't eat me!" cried Middle Billy Goat Gruff. "Wait for my brother, Big Billy Goat Gruff. He is **MUCH** bigger than me."

The troll scratched his head and thought for a minute. "**OH, ALRIGHT,**" he grumbled. "**BUT YOU HAD BETTER GET OFF MY BRIDGE BEFORE I CHANGE MY MIND**!"

Later in the day, Big Billy Goat Gruff started across the stone bridge. TRIP-TRAP! TRIP-TRAP! went his heavy hoofs on the bridge. The bridge began to creak and groan. The noise woke up the sleeping troll.

"**WHO'S THAT WALKING ACROSS MY BRIDGE?**" shouted the troll.

"**IT IS I, BIG BILLY GOAT GRUFF,**" said the goat in a deep loud voice.

"**I'VE BEEN WAITING FOR YOU!**" shouted the troll happily. "**I'M COMING UP THERE AND I'M GOING TO GOBBLE YOU UP!**"

"**COME AHEAD,**" shouted Big Billy Goat Gruff. "**I'M NOT AFRAID OF YOU, MR. TROLL!**"

So the troll climbed onto the bridge and stared at Big Billy Goat Gruff in an angry way.

Big Billy Goat Gruff stared back at the ugly old troll. He scraped his one front hoof in an angry way. Then Big Billy Goat Gruff lowered his horns and **CHARGED!** He butted the troll as hard as he could. The troll flew high up into the sky and sailed out of sight! Mr. Troll was never heard of or seen again.

Big Billy Goat Gruff trip-trapped proudly across the bridge and joined his brothers in the meadow.

The Gruff Brothers jumped and danced about happily and sang,

"Hip, hip, hooray!
The troll's gone away.
Now we can munch
On green grass for lunch
Every bright and sunny day.
Hip, hip, hooray!"

The Three Billy Goats Gruff

Answer each question with a good sentence.

1. Which character in the story was the villain? Tell why.
   _____
   _____

2. Which characters in the story had to pretend they were brave?
   _____
   _____

3. Which character in the story was brave and clever? Tell why.
   _____
   _____

4. Do you think the troll was tricked by the goats? Tell how.
   _____
   _____

5. How would the story have been different if the goats were all the same size?
   _____
   _____

6. What other animals, besides goats, could have been in the story? Tell why.
   _____
   _____

Fairy Tale 4: Phonics - Review of "r" blends

The Three Billy Goats Gruff

Many words in the story begin with an "r" blend.

The blend may be br, cr, dr, gr, fr, tr, or pr.

Read each clue and look for the word in the story that begins with an "r" blend. Print the word on the line.

1. It was something that grew in a meadow. _____

2. The goats must walk on it to get to the meadow. _____

3. It was ugly and grumpy and the goats were afraid of it. _____

4. The sound the goats made as they walked on the bridge. _____

5. It is the color of the grass in the meadow. _____

6. Big Billy Goat Gruff walked this way across the bridge. _____

7. The bridge made these sounds. _____ _____

8. It is the Billy Goats' last name. _____

Fairy Tale 4: Word Study - Rhyming Words, Alphabetical Order, Antonyms

The Three Billy Goats Gruff

A. The words "bluff" and "gruff" rhyme.

Beside each word print a rhyming word on the line.

1. goat _____   4. three _____   7. trap _____

2. gruff _____   5. grumpy _____   8. cross _____

3. Billy _____   6. trip _____   9. horn _____

B. Copy each group of words in the correct alphabetical order.

1. bridge, billy, butted, big _____

2. troll, tiny, trap, trip _____

3. goats, gruff, gobble, grass _____

4. straggly, saucers, second, strong _____

C. The three **thin** goats ate the good green grass to get **fat**.

The words "thin" and "fat" are opposites.

Beside each word print its <u>opposite</u> on the line.

1. tiny _____   6. loud _____

2. ugly _____   7. over _____

3. roared _____   8. kind _____

4. started _____   9. big _____

5. light _____   10. in _____

The Three Billy Goats Gruff

Choose one of the titles from the list and write a new story about the Three Billy Goats Gruff or the Troll.

1. The Three Billy Goats and the Dragon

2. The Three Billy Goats and the Wolf

3. The Return of the Troll

4. The Three Trolls and the Grumpy Goats

5. The Troll's Trick

The Little Red Hen

Once upon a time there was a Little Red Hen. She lived in a small cottage with her ten little chicks. The Little Red Hen worked hard all day long looking for food to feed her family. All day she went about the cottage singing as she worked.

One day, the Little Red Hen went out for a walk with her friends, the goose, the cat, and the pig. While she was walking, she found some grains of wheat. She decided to plant the grains in the ground.

"Who will help to plant this wheat?" the Little Red Hen asked her friends, the goose, the cat, and the pig.

"**Not I!**" said the goose honking loudly.

"**Not I!**" said the cat meowing in a soft voice.

"**Not I!**" oinked and grunted the pig.

"Then I will plant it myself," said the Little Red Hen proudly. And she did. She dug holes in the dirt and placed the seeds inside and then covered them up. The Little Red Hen watered them and hoped they would grow.

Every day the Little Red Hen watered and checked her seeds. One morning she saw green leaves peeking out of the dirt.

"Oh, come and see the green wheat growing!" she called to her chicks. "Soon we will have some wheat to make flour." Her little chicks came running over to see the wheat growing.

All summer long the wheat grew taller and taller. It turned from green to gold. At last it was time to cut the wheat.

The Little Red Hen called to her friends.

"Who will help me cut this wheat?" the Little Red Hen asked her friends, the goose, the cat, and the pig.

"**Not I!**" honked the goose with her beak in the air.

"**Not I!**" said the cat as she washed her paws.

"**Not I!**" oinked the pig as he rolled in the mud.

"Then, I will do it all by myself," said the Little Red Hen. And she did.

When the wheat was all cut down, it was time for it to be threshed. The Little Red Hen called to her friends.

"Who will help me thresh this wheat" she asked her friends, the goose, the cat, and the pig.

"**Not I!**" honked the goose as it waddled away.

"**Not I!**" meowed the cat as it tried to catch a mouse.

"**Not I!**" grunted the pig as he chewed on an apple.

"Then I will do it myself," said the Little Red Hen. And she did.

When the wheat was threshed the Little Red Hen poured the golden grains into a huge sack. The next morning the Little Red Hen planned to take the seeds to the mill to have them ground into flour. She asked her friends, the goose, the cat, and the pig, "Who will help me take this wheat to the mill to be ground into flour?"

"**Not I!**" honked the goose while she pecked at the ground.

"**Not I!**" hissed the cat in an angry voice.

"**Not I!**" snorted the pig while he drank some water.

"Then I guess I will have to do it myself," said the Little Red Hen. And that is what she did.

The next day, the Little Red Hen decided to bake some bread. She asked her friends, the goose, the cat, and the pig, "Who will help me make this flour into a lovely loaf of bread?"

"**Not I!**" honked the goose again.

"**Not I!**" meowed the cat again.

"**Not I!**" oinked the pig again.

"Then I guess I will have to do it all by myself," said the Little Red Hen. And that is what she did.

At last the bread was baked and the Little Red Hen called to her friends, the goose, the cat, and the pig. She asked, "Who will help me eat this lovely loaf of bread?"

"**I will!**" honked the goose happily.

"**I will!**" purred the cat in a sweet voice.

"**I will!**" oinked the pig hungrily.

The three friends quickly ran to the Little Red Hen's cottage. When they got there the Little Red Hen said "**Oh, no you won't!** I found the wheat and I planted it. I watched the wheat grow. When it was ready I cut it and threshed it. Then I took it to the mill to be ground into flour and made it into a lovely loaf of bread. Now my chicks and I shall have a delicious lunch." And they did.

Fairy Tale 5: Reading Comprehension - Recalling Events, Making Inferences

The Little Red Hen

Answer each question with a good sentence.

1. Who were the characters in the story?

2. What did the Little Red Hen find one day?

3. What did the Little Red Hen do with the grains of wheat?

4. What did the Little Red Hen ask her friends?

5. Why didn't the Little Red Hen share her bread with her friends?

6. Do you think the Little Red Hen treated her friends fairly? Tell why.

7. Would you like to have friends like the goose, the cat, and the pig? Tell why.

Fairy Tale 5: Phonics - Short Vowel "e"

The Little Red Hen

The words "red" and "hen" have the short vowel "e" sound.

Color only the pictures that have the same vowel sound as red and hen.

Fairy Tale 5: Word Study - Word Family "ake"

The Little Red Hen

Working With the "ake" Word Family

A. Make new words using "ake".

1. dr + ake = _____
2. c + ake = _____
3. sn + ake = _____
4. r + ake = _____
5. fl + ake = _____
6. sh + ake = _____
7. l + ake = _____
8. w + ake = _____

B. Use the words that you made to complete these sentences.

1. A big white snow _____ fell on my nose.
2. The little green _____ hid under a plant in the garden.
3. The _____ was too cold for swimming.
4. In the autumn, I like to _____ the leaves into piles.
5. On Billy's birthday _____ there were seven blue candles.
6. A _____ is the name for a male duck.
7. _____ up, Joey, it is time for you to go to school.
8. A bird will _____ its wet feathers to dry them.

Fairy Tale 5: Creative Thinking - Brainstorming and Illustrating

The Little Red Hen

The Little Red Hen used the flour to make some bread.

Think of other things that she could make with the flour.

Print the word and draw a picture for each one.

She could make _____.	She could make _____.
She could make _____.	She could make _____.
She could make _____.	She could make _____.

Fairy Tale 6

The Gingerbread Man

Once upon a time, in a little cottage, lived an old lady and an old man. They did not have any children of their own and were lonely.

One day, the little old lady was making some gingerbread cookies. "I think I'll make a gingerbread man," she said to herself. She cut the gingerbread dough into the shape of a little boy and decorated it. The little old lady gave the gingerbread man eyes and a nose made out of raisins and a mouth made of pink frosting. Down the middle of his body were three red cherries for buttons.

The little old lady put the gingerbread man into the oven to bake. Soon there was a spicy smell throughout the little cottage.

When the gingerbread man was baked, the little old lady opened the oven door. Suddenly, out jumped the gingerbread man. As he ran out of the door to the cottage he called,

**"Run, run, as fast as you can!
You can't catch me,
For I'm the gingerbread man."**

The little old lady and the little old man tried to catch him but soon the gingerbread man was out of sight.

Fairy Tale 6 — The Gingerbread Man

The gingerbread man came to a field where some men were cutting hay. "Stop, little gingerbread man," called the men. "We want to eat you."

"Oh, ho!" laughed the little gingerbread man. "I ran away from a little old lady and a little old man, and I can run away from you, too!"

> **"Run, run, as fast as you can!**
> **You can't catch me,**
> **For I'm the gingerbread man!"**

Along the way, the gingerbread man came to a horse standing under a tree. "Stop, little gingerbread man," called the horse. "You look good enough to eat."

"Oh, ho!" laughed the gingerbread man. "I ran away from a little old lady, a little old man, and some men cutting hay, and I can run away from you, too."

> **"Run, run, as fast as you can!**
> **You can't catch me,**
> **For I'm the gingerbread man!"**

Soon the gingerbread man came to a fat brown cow looking over a fence chewing some grass. "Stop, little gingerbread man," called the fat brown cow. "You look good enough to eat!"

"Oh, ho!" laughed the gingerbread man. "I ran away from a little old lady, a little old man, some men cutting hay, and a horse. I can run away from you, too!"

> **"Run, run, as fast as you can!
> You can't catch me,
> For I'm the gingerbread man!"**

The gingerbread man ran until he came to a stream. "How will I ever get across?" said the gingerbread man to himself.

Near the stream sat a sly old fox. He saw the gingerbread man looking at the stream. "M-m-m-m, what a tasty snack he would make," the fox said to himself.

The fox walked over to the gingerbread man and said, "Let me help you cross the stream. I can swim across with you sitting on my tail. Come on, jump on my tail before it's too late." And that's what the gingerbread man did.

So off they went across the stream. As the water got deeper, the fox called out, "If you are getting wet, jump onto my back." And that's what the gingerbread man did.

In the middle of the stream, the gingerbread man called out, "Please help me, my legs are getting wet."

The fox said, "Then jump on my head as it is higher and you won't get wet."

The gingerbread man climbed up on top of the fox's head and stood between his ears.

"Why don't you come closer and sit on my nose?" said the fox. "You will not get wet there."

The gingerbread man got up and went down to sit near the fox's nose. Suddenly there was a big **SNAP** and the fox gobbled him up in one big bite! He licked his lips and said, "Oh my, what a tasty afternoon snack you made, little gingerbread man!"

And that was the end of the gingerbread man.

Fairy Tale 6: Reading Comprehension - Recalling Details, Making Inferences

The Gingerbread Man

Answer each question with a good sentence.

1. What did the old lady bake one day?

2. How did her gingerbread man look?

3. What happened when the old lady opened the oven door?

4. Who was the gingerbread man able to run away from? List their names in the correct order.

5. Which character in the story was very clever?

6. How did the fox prove he was very clever?

Fairy Tale 6: Phonics - Soft Gg, Hard Gg

The Gingerbread Man

The letter "g" makes two sounds. In the word **good** the "g" makes a hard sound. In the word **ginger** the "g" makes a soft sound. In the big box below are some pictures. Color the pictures that have the soft "g" sound blue. Color the pictures that have the hard "g" sound red.

Fairy Tale 6: Word Study - Syllabication, Compound Words

The Gingerbread Man

A. A syllable is a word part. Some words have <u>one</u> syllable, some have <u>two</u> syllables, and some have <u>three</u>.

Record the number of syllables that you hear in each word on the line.

1. cottage ____
2. gingerbread ____
3. raisins ____
4. across ____
5. suddenly ____
6. stream ____
7. afternoon ____
8. snack ____

B. The word gingerbread is a <u>compound</u> word.

A compound word is made of two smaller words. Example: ginger+bread

Use the words in the gingerbread man to make compound words.

1. _____
2. _____
3. _____
4. _____
5. _____
6. _____
7. _____
8. _____

Fairy Tale: Creative Thinking - Illustrating

The Gingerbread Man

Decorate your own gingerbread man. Make him look yummy!

The Gingerbread Man

Write a story about your gingerbread man.

The Ugly Duckling

Once upon a time, near some water, a mother duck made a nest. In the nest she laid six eggs. Five of the eggs were the same size. One was very big with a bumpy shell. Mother Duck sat on the eggs every day to keep the eggs warm.

"How much longer will it be?" Mother Duck asked herself. She kept waiting for the little taps that told her the ducklings were ready to come out of their shells.

One day, the five smaller eggs began to crack open. Out popped five fluffy, yellow ducklings. They began peeping as they came out. Mother Duck was glad. She began to quack happily at her ducklings.

Mother Duck was very proud of her ducklings and wanted to show them off to the other birds that lived near the pond. She wanted to take them for a walk. She looked back in the nest to check to see if all her ducklings were behind her. It was then that she saw that the big bumpy egg had not cracked open. Mother Duck went back to her nest and sat on it longer. After a few more days, the shell began to crack and out tumbled a big ugly gray duckling with a long neck.

"Oh, my!" said Mother Duck. "What kind of bird is this?"

Mother Duck knew that this duckling was not the same as her other ducklings. Even her own ducklings asked her why their brother looked so different. She tried to protect him but the other ducklings and birds pecked at him. They called him names and chased him away.

The ugly duckling was so unhappy and lonely. No one liked him and he was tired of being pecked and called names. "I will run away!" cried the ugly duckling. "No one likes me here! I am going to look for a new pond or lake where I can live happily."

The ugly duckling decided to look for a place where no one knew him. He traveled until he found a large marsh. The wild geese and ducks who lived there made him feel welcome.

"What kind of bird are you?" asked the geese kindly. "You don't look like one of us but that is alright. You may stay with us for as long as you like." The geese then swam away and left him alone to look for food and a place to sleep. The ugly duckling spent his days swimming about the marsh happily.

Soon autumn came. The air was cooler and the leaves on the trees fell to the ground. One day, the ugly duckling saw a flock of beautiful birds with huge, white wings flying south over the marsh. As he watched them he cried out, "I wish I was as pretty as those birds." The ugly duckling did not know that the birds were swans.

Soon winter came to the marsh. The winds grew colder. The water in the lake became frozen and the ugly duckling had no place to swim. He had to find a place to stay for the winter so he walked to some nearby woods. In the woods he found a hiding place under some bushes. Here he made a nest for himself. The ugly duckling spent many days in his nest as the snow fell silently outside.

During the winter, the ugly duckling found it hard to find food and was always hungry. He could never keep warm as it was always cold in his nest. One day, he saw that his feathers were beginning to fall out. The duckling used them to line his nest to help keep him warm. He worried about losing his feathers as he was afraid that this would make him look even uglier than he was before.

In the spring, a whole year had passed. The warm sun shone. The grass became soft and green. Birds sang in the trees and the smell of flowers was in the air. The duckling was very happy. The days were warm and the ice melted on the marsh. He could swim and look for food again.

After a while, the duckling soon found that he was the only one swimming about the marsh. This made him feel sad and lonely. He forgot that all the other birds had gone south for the winter. He hoped they would return soon.

One day, the ugly duckling spread his wings to fly over the marsh. He was so surprised to find how strong his wings were. As he was flying he saw two beautiful swans swimming on the marsh. He watched them as they floated gracefully on the water. Oh, how he wished he was like them. The ugly duckling decided to fly down to swim near them.

The duckling landed on the water nearby and swam toward the swans. As the duckling got close he bowed his head waiting for the swans to call him names. When he looked down into the water he saw another graceful swan floating on the water. It was his own reflection.

He was no longer a clumsy, ugly duckling. He was a swan. His gray ugly feathers had dropped off and now his feathers were white and shiny. He had a long graceful neck and powerful wings.

"I am beautiful, like you," he whispered to the other swans.

The swans floated over to meet him and rubbed his neck with their beaks. They were telling the new swan that they liked him. At last the lonely duckling knew where he belonged.

Fairy Tale 7: Reading Comprehension - Observing Sequence

The Ugly Duckling

When did it happen in the story?

Print the word "before" or "after" or "during" in each sentence.

1. The ugly duckling ran away _____ the other birds pecked him and teased him.

2. The duckling changed into a swan _____ the winter.

3. Mother Duck made a nest _____ she laid her eggs.

4. The ugly duckling knew he was a swan _____ he looked in the water.

5. The ugly duckling made a nest in the woods _____ the marsh had ice on it.

6. _____ the winter the duckling was cold and hungry.

7. The five small eggs hatched _____ the big bumpy egg.

8. The air was cooler and the trees lost their leaves _____ the autumn.

9. The swans were flying south _____ winter came.

10. The duckling was lonely and sad _____ the spring on the marsh.

Fairy Tale 7: Phonics - Short "u" Vowel Sound

The Ugly Duckling

The <u>short</u> "u" sound is heard in the words "ugly" and "duckling". Color <u>only</u> the eggs that have words with the short "u" sound.

bumpy	south	hungry
about	rubbed	June
fluffy	use	jump
shout	duck	push
tune	turtle	cube

Fairy Tale 7: Word Study - Using Comparisons

The Ugly Duckling

Color in the circle beside the word that fits the sentence. Print the word on the line.

1. The bumpy egg was the _____ one in the nest.

   ○ big   ○ bigger   ○ biggest

2. Five of the eggs were _____ than the bumpy egg.

   ○ small   ○ smaller   ○ smallest

3. Mother Duck had to sit on the big egg the _____.

   ○ long   ○ longer   ○ longest

4. The duckling's gray feathers became white and _____.

   ○ shiny   ○ shinier   ○ shiniest

5. The wind was _____ in the autumn at the marsh.

   ○ cool   ○ cooler   ○ coolest

6. The _____ duckling had gray feathers and a long neck.

   ○ ugly   ○ uglier   ○ ugliest

7. The days got _____ in the spring and the ice melted.

   ○ warm   ○ warmer   ○ warmest

8. Winter at the marsh was very _____ and the water became ice.

   ○ cold   ○ colder   ○ coldest

Fairy Tale 7: Creative Thinking - Illustrating Sentences

The Ugly Duckling

How did the ugly duckling look in each sentence?

Draw a picture to show how it looked and color it neatly.

One of the eggs was big and bumpy.	The shell cracked open and out tumbled a big, gray, ugly duckling.
The ugly duckling sat in its nest during the cold winter.	The ugly duckling was now a beautiful swan.

Fairy Tale 8

The Elves and the Shoemaker

Once upon a time, in a little village, lived a shoemaker and his wife. They lived in two rooms at the back of the shoemaker's shop.

The shoemaker had grown old. His eyesight was weak and his fingers stitched the shoes slowly. He could no longer make shoes as fast as before. The shoemaker and his wife were getting poorer and poorer.

One day, the shoemaker discovered that he only had enough leather for one more pair of shoes. That evening, he cut the leather into pieces and laid them on his workbench. He decided to finish making the shoes the next morning and went to bed.

The next morning, the shoemaker and his wife came into the workshop to find a very nice surprise. On the shoemaker's workbench sat the finest pair of shoes that he and his wife had ever seen. He picked up the shoes and he stared at them in wonder. The shoes were perfectly sewn.

"My dear," the shoemaker said to his wife. "Did you come into the shop and make these shoes during the night?"

"No," she replied. "I did not."

"Well, I did not make them. I wonder who did?" said the shoemaker.

Later that day, a rich man came into the shop to buy a pair of shoes. The shoemaker showed him the new shoes. The rich man liked them very much and paid the shoemaker five pieces of gold.

Now the shoemaker could buy enough leather for two more pairs of shoes. That night he cut out the leather and left the pieces on his workbench again. Then he went to bed.

On his workbench, the next morning, the shoemaker found two more pairs of neatly stitched shoes. This time they were shoes that ladies would like.

"How could this be?" said the shoemaker to his wife.

Before his wife could answer two ladies walked in.

"Good day," one of the ladies said. "My husband came in yesterday and bought a pair of beautiful shoes. My sister and I would like to find something as well."

The shoemaker showed the new shoes to the two ladies. They tried on the newly made shoes and found that they fit perfectly.

"Goodness," said the one lady, "These are delightful! I'll tell everyone I know to visit your shop."

For nights the same thing happened. The leather that the shoemaker had cut out was mysteriously sewn and made into shoes. The shoemaker's shop soon became a very busy place as many people came to buy his wonderful shoes. The shoemaker and his wife were no longer poor.

One day the shoemaker said to his wife, "We must find out who is helping us. Let's stay up late and hide to see who is making these shoes."

That night, the shoemaker and his wife decided to hide in a dark corner of the workshop. Suddenly they heard a sound. At midnight, out came three little elves who wore no clothes. They climbed up on the workbench and set to work stitching, sewing, and hammering. How fast their little fingers flew!

The shoemaker and his wife couldn't believe their eyes.

"Why, it's elves!" said the shoemaker's wife. "But look! They do not have any clothes or shoes. They work so hard for us they do not have time to make things for themselves."

The elves didn't stop working until all of the shoes were done. Then they jumped down from the workbench and disappeared out of the shop.

The next day, the shoemaker and his wife wanted to do something nice for their little friends. They decided to make things for them to wear. The shoemaker made each elf a pair of little shoes. His wife decided to sew each elf a pair of trousers, a shirt, and a jacket. She was also going to knit each elf a pair of socks and a hat.

The shoemaker and his wife worked all day long on the clothes and shoes. At last they were finished. They laid the tiny clothes out on the shoemaker's workbench. When it was dark the shoemaker and his wife hid in a corner of the workshop to wait for the elves.

At midnight, the elves returned. Quickly, they climbed up on the shoemaker's workbench. They were ready to work on the piles of leather pieces that the shoemaker always left. What a surprise they had! There on the workbench were tiny sets of new clothes and new shoes.

Excitedly they tried on the clothes. They were so happy that they began to dance and sing.

**"Look at us!
Don't we look neat!
Now we have clothes
To keep us warm,
And shoes upon our feet!"**

The elves sang and danced around the workbench and to the door of the shop. They opened the door and disappeared into the dark of the night.

The shoemaker and his wife smiled at each other and then went to bed happy and pleased. Even though the elves never returned to the shoemaker's shop, the shoemaker and his wife had good fortune for the rest of their lives.

The Elves and the Shoemaker

Answer each question with a good sentence.

1. Why were the shoemaker and his wife so poor?
   _____
   _____

2. Where do you think the elves stayed during the day?
   _____
   _____

3. Why do you think the elves only came out at night?
   _____
   _____
   _____

4. How do you think the elves knew the shoemaker needed their help?
   _____
   _____

5. How did the shoemaker and his wife find out who was making the shoes?
   _____
   _____

6. How did the shoemaker and his wife thank the elves for all their help?
   _____
   _____

Fairy Tale 8: Phonics - Sh Digraph

The Elves and the Shoemaker

The shoemaker made shoes for the elves.

The words "shoes" and "shoemaker" begin with the sound that "sh" makes.

Cut out the pictures that begin with "sh" and paste them on the elf's shoe.

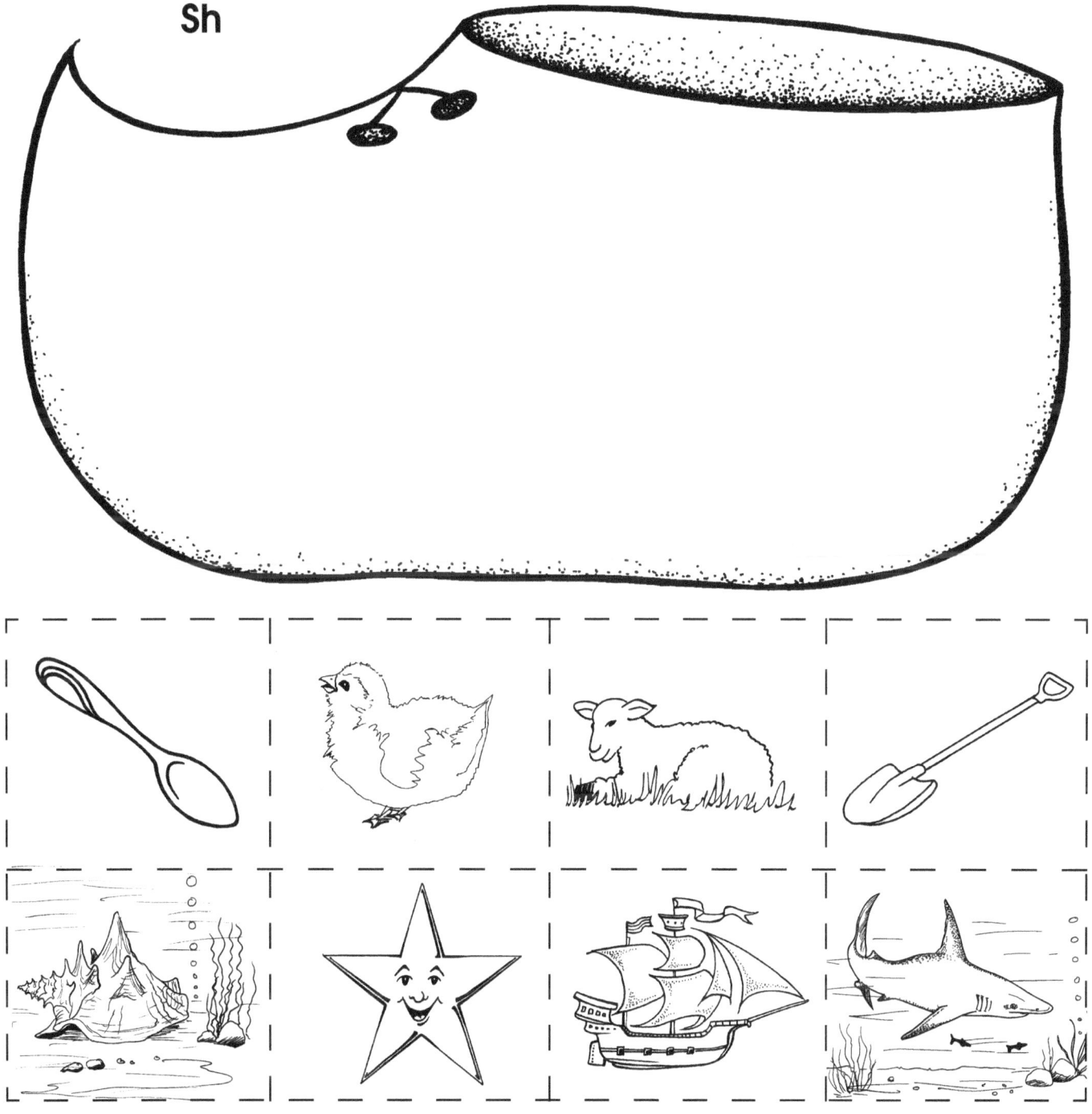

Fairy Tale 8: Word Study - Word Meanings

The Elves and the Shoemaker

Crossword Puzzle Fun!

Word Bank

shoemaker	poor	midnight	workbench
shoes	slowly	leather	shop
finished	stitched		

Across

1. all done
2. used to make shoes
3. a place to work
4. something to wear
5. opposite to rich

Down

1. middle of the night
2. opposite to quickly
3. a man who makes shoes
4. sewn together
5. a kind of store

Fairy Tale 8: Creative Writing - Writing a Letter and a Story

The Elves and the Shoemaker

A. Pretend that you are the shoemaker. Write a thank you letter to the elves.

Dear _____,

_____
_____
_____
_____
_____
_____

B. Write a story about an elf. Try to use the words in the shape in your story.

elf
pot
shoes
small
gold
wish
green
magic
dance
tricks
suit
hid

The Four Musicians

There was once a donkey who had worked hard for his master for many years. He was getting too old to work so his master was going to sell him at the market. The donkey decided to run away to a nearby town. He was going to become a musician in the town band.

The next day, the donkey pushed open the door to the barn and walked down the road to town. Along the way, he found a sad-looking dog lying on the side of the road.

"Hello, dog," said the donkey. "Why do you look so sad?"

The dog looked at the donkey and said, "My master does not want me to watch over his house any more. I am too old and nearly blind. He was going to get rid of me, so I ran away."

"Come with me," said the donkey. "I am going to town to become a musician. I can bray very loudly."

The dog said, "I'll go with you as I can bark loudly and howl sadly. My bark and howl are very musical and will help the band." So the two runaways set off together down the road.

Before long they met a sad-looking cat who was sitting on the branch of a large tree.

"Why are you so sad and unhappy, cat?" asked the donkey.

"My master kicked me out of his house because I am not fast enough to catch mice any more," said the cat. "I don't know what I am going to do next."

"Why don't you join us?" said the donkey. "We're going to town to join the town band."

"I would be glad to join you. I can help to make good music with my purring and meowing in the town band."

So off down the road went the three animals. Along the way they met an old rooster sitting on a fence. He was crowing very sadly.

"What is wrong with your cock-a-doodle-doo?" asked the donkey. "It sounds very sad."

"Oh, I am not as young as I used to be," said the rooster. "My owner told the cook to get an axe to chop off my head. She wanted me cooked for her dinner so I ran away."

"Come with us to town," said the donkey. "You have a good voice to add to the town band."

Along the way to town the four musicians sang at the tops of their voices. The donkey brayed, the dog barked, the cat meowed, and the rooster crowed cock-a-doodle-doo. The animals were pleased with their music.

When night came the animals found themselves at the edge of a large forest. They decided to spend the night there. The donkey, the dog, and the cat lay under the tree. The rooster sat on the highest branch and looked about.

"I can see a light shining in the forest. There must be a house close by," called the rooster to his friends.

"Let's find that house," said the donkey. "It would be better to spend the night in a house than under a tree."

All the animals agreed with the donkey and set off to find the house deep in the forest. Soon they saw the house with the light and walked quietly towards it. When they got close enough to it the donkey, who was the tallest animal, looked in the window.

"What do you see?" whispered the dog.

"I see a fire burning in the fireplace. There is a table full of things to eat and drink. Around the table are some mean robbers sitting and eating," said the donkey softly.

"It's inside the house we want to be," said the rooster softly. "If we get rid of the robbers we could have a home of our own."

The four animals thought of ways to get rid of the robbers. At last, they came up with a plan. As soon as the light in the house went out, the animals began to make their music. The donkey brayed hee-haw, hee-haw. The cat meowed loudly. The dog barked and growled angrily. The rooster crowed cock-a-doodle-doo as loud as he could. What a frightening sound they all made!

Then the donkey kicked in the window and the animals all rushed into the house. The cat hissed and scratched the robbers while the rooster pecked at their heads. The dog bit their legs and the donkey kicked about wildly. The robbers jumped out of their beds and tried to get out of the house. They had a terrible time trying not to be scratched, bitten, pecked, or kicked by this terrible monster that had entered their house. They were so scared that they ran into the forest and were never seen again.

The four musicians were happy in their new home. They liked their own band and the music that they made. They decided to stay in the house and make it their new home. Maybe they are still making their music today.

Fairy Tale 9: Reading Comprehension - Recalling Details

The Four Musicians

Answer each question with a good sentence.

1. Who were the main characters in the story?
   _____
   _____

2. Why were the animals running away from their homes?
   _____
   _____

3. Why did their owners want to get rid of them?
   _____
   _____

4. Do you think the animals were treated fairly by their masters? Tell why.
   _____
   _____
   _____

5. How did the animals chase the robbers away?
   _____
   _____
   _____

6. Why did the robbers run away and never come back to the house?
   _____
   _____

The Four Musicians

Use the rhyming pairs in the word box to complete each rhyming couplet.

| see | mouse | unkind | old | light | hound | today |
| tree | house | blind | sold | night | found | say |

1. The donkey's master was taking him to be _____
   At a market because he was getting too _____.

2. At the side of the road the donkey _____
   A very sad-looking dog who was a _____.

3. The dog's master was very _____,
   As his dog was old and almost _____.

4. The sad-faced cat was kicked out of the _____,
   Because he could not catch a little _____.

5. The old rooster overheard his master _____,
   I want him cooked for my dinner _____.

6. The animals slept under the big _____.
   The rooster sat up high so he could _____.

7. In the dark forest late that _____,
   The rooster could see a little white _____.

Fairy Tale 9: Word Study - Understanding Feelings

The Four Musicians

The words in the box are used to tell feelings.

angry	curious	happy	tired
annoyed	excited	pleased	unhappy
cross	frightened	surprised	worried

Answer each question with a feeling word or words. The character may have felt more than one way.

1. How do you think the donkey felt when he knew his master was going to sell him?
   _____

2. How do you think the donkey's master might have felt when he found the donkey gone?
   _____

3. How do you think the dog, the cat, and the rooster felt when the donkey wanted them to come with him?
   _____

4. How might the mouse have felt when the cat could not catch him?
   _____

5. How might the animals have felt when they heard their voices together?
   _____

6. How do you think the robbers felt when they heard the noise outside the window?
   _____

Fairy Tale 9: Creative Thinking - Illustrating; Listing Adjectives

The Four Musicians

The robbers thought a terrible monster had come into their house one night. Draw a picture of this monster and color it neatly.

On the lines make a list of words that describe the monster.
_____
_____
_____
_____

Jack and the Beanstalk

Once upon a time a silly boy named Jack and his mother lived in a little cottage. They were very poor. All they had was a cow that gave them milk. Jack and his mother used the milk to make butter and cheese to sell at the market. The money they got was used to buy food.

One day the cow stopped giving them milk. Jack's mother told Jack to take the cow to the market to sell it. Away went Jack down the road pulling the cow behind him. Along the way he met an old man. The man told Jack he would give him a bag of magic beans for the cow. Now, Jack did not like walking to the market on a hot day so he decided to take the bag of magic beans.

Jack hurried home to show his mother the magic beans. When Jack's mother saw them, she became very angry. She grabbed the bag and threw the beans out the window. She then sent Jack to bed without any supper.

The next morning, when Jack woke up, part of his room was in darkness. He jumped out of bed and ran to the window. Standing near his house was a huge beanstalk. Jack quickly dressed and ran outside and began to climb it. Above the clouds he found a shining white road. Jack followed the road to a huge castle and knocked on the door. A very tall woman opened it. She was the giant's wife.

"Good morning," said Jack. "I am very hungry. Will you give me something to eat?"

"What?" cried the woman. "Don't you know that my husband is a giant and lives in this castle? If he sees you he will eat you."

"Oh, please," begged Jack. "I have come a long way and I am very hungry. I will be gone before the giant returns."

"Alright, come inside but please be quick," said the giant's wife.

In the kitchen, she gave Jack a bowl of porridge. Suddenly they heard a loud noise. **Thump! Thump!** The giant was coming home for his breakfast. The woman told Jack to hide in the oven. When the giant came into the kitchen he shouted in a such a very loud voice that Jack began to shiver and shake.

"Fee-fi-fo-fum! I smell the blood of an Englishman!" shouted the giant at his wife.

"It's just the meat that I have cooked for you," said his wife. "Sit down and I will give you some."

The giant sat down at the big table. His wife gave him his breakfast and he ate all of it. After his meal the giant took out three bags of gold and began to count the coins from one of them. He became sleepy from his big meal and before long he was fast asleep.

Jack climbed out of the oven and grabbed one of the bags of gold and ran out of the castle to his home. When he gave the bag of gold to his mother she cried, "We are no longer poor! The beans were magic after all!"

When there were only a few pieces of gold left, Jack climbed the beanstalk a second time. This time when the giant's wife opened the door she did not see Jack slip between her legs and sneak into the castle. He hid in the oven again and waited for the giant to return. In a little while the giant came in shouting, **"Fee-fi-fo-fum! I smell the blood of an Englishman."**

His wife told him there was no one there and to sit down and eat his lunch that was waiting for him on the table. After the giant ate his lunch he asked his wife to bring his magic hen. She put the big brown hen on the table in front of the giant. The giant shouted at the hen to lay a golden egg. When the giant saw the golden egg, he clapped his hands happily and asked the hen to do it again. Before long the giant fell asleep.

Jack jumped out of the oven and grabbed the magic hen, Quickly he ran to the beanstalk and climbed down it. Jack ran into the house and showed his mother the magic hen and told it to lay a golden egg. "Oh, Jack!" cried his mother. "We will never have to worry about money again as we are rich!"

A few months later Jack decided to climb the beanstalk again. This time, Jack did not knock at the door of the castle. He went inside quietly and hid in a cupboard near the door.

Before long, the castle began to shake and quake as the giant was returning home. He shouted again, **"Fee-fi-fo-fum! I smell the blood of an Englishman."**

"You are silly," said his wife. "There is no one here but you and me. Now, sit down and eat your dinner." So the giant sat down and ate. After he had eaten, he asked his wife to bring his silver harp. The giant told the harp to sing. At once the harp sang a beautiful song which put the giant to sleep.

Jack jumped out of the cupboard, grabbed the harp and ran out of the castle and down the road to the beanstalk as fast as he could. The giant woke up when he heard the harp calling for help and ran after Jack.

Jack quickly climbed down the beanstalk. At the bottom he looked up and could see the giant coming after him. He ran into the house to get an ax to chop down the beanstalk. As he was chopping the beanstalk suddenly cracked and broke. The giant and the beanstalk came crashing down to the ground.

The giant was dead. Jack and his mother lived happily ever after. They were no longer poor and had a harp that played beautiful music.

Fairy Tale 10: Reading Comprehension - Character Analysis

Jack and the Beanstalk

In the story there are four main characters.

Read the words in the cloud and use them to describe each character.

Record the words under each character's name. The words may be used more than once.

ugly, man, worried, woman, sleepy, bully, small, old, hungry, young, mean, huge, smart, king, unhappy, kind, big, boy, scary, grumpy, loud, silly, curious, brave, caring

Giant

_____
_____
_____
_____

Giant's Wife

_____
_____
_____
_____

Jack

_____
_____
_____
_____

Jack's Mother

_____
_____
_____
_____

Fairy Tale 10: Phonics - Long and Short Vowels

Jack and the Beanstalk

Print the missing vowel sound in each word.

1. thr __ e b _ gs of g __ ld

2. __ gly g __ __ nt

3. a h __ ge c __ stle

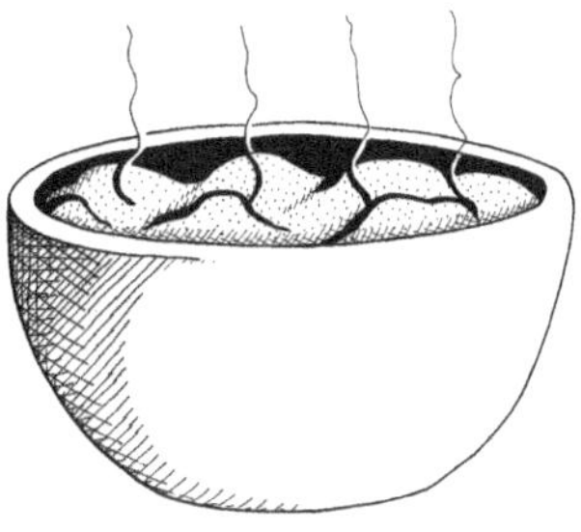

4. a h __ t b __ wl of p __ rr __ dge

5. a g __ ld __ n __ gg

6. a s __ ng __ ng s __ lver h __ rp

7. a m __ g __ c h __ n

8. a b __ g b __ anst __ lk

Fairy Tale 10: Word Study - Antonyms, Synonyms, Compound Words

Jack and the Beanstalk

A. Look in the story to find a word that means the opposite to each word below. Print it on the line beside it.

1. night _____
2. small _____
3. slowly _____
4. soft _____

5. whispered _____
6. before _____
7. awake _____
8. short _____

B. Look in the story to find a word that means the same as each word below. Print it on the line beside it.

1. yelled _____
2. rap _____
3. palace _____
4. foolish _____

5. house _____
6. come back _____
7. took _____
8. lad _____

C. A compound word is a big word made of two words. Look in the story for compound words. Print them on the lines below.

_____

_____

_____

Fairy Tale 10: Creative Thinking - Writing a Story

Jack and the Beanstalk

Draw a picture of your own giant and write a story about it.

In your story tell:

- what he looks like
- what he is like
- where he lives
- how he acts
- what he wears
- the food that he likes

Try to use some of these words in your story:

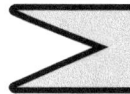

stupid	large	one-eyed	grumpy	clumsy	beard
club	friendly	hairy	toothless	castle	kind
big	ugly	mean	stomps	thumps	yells
tall	selfish	cave	pounds	greedy	shouts

My Giant

Fairy Tale Creative Activities

Creative Activity 1

Fairy Tale Puppet Play

Choose the fairy tale that you liked the best.

Plan a puppet play with some classmates.

Make paper bag puppets for the characters in the story.

Practice your play and put it on for the class.

. . . .

Creative Activity 2

Fairy Tale Poster

Choose your favorite fairy tale.

Make a poster telling something about the story.

Put the title of the fairy tale at the top of your poster.

Draw a colorful picture of the part that you liked the best.

. . . .

Creative Activity 3

Fairy Tale Villain

In many fairy tales there is often a bad character called a villain.

Think of other fairy tales that have bad characters or villains.

Try to draw pictures of six villains and print their names.

Creative Activity 4

Character Models

Choose your favorite fairy tale.

Using Plasticine or modeling clay, model the characters from the story.

Make name cards for each one.

Place your characters in a display box.

....

Creative Activity 5

My Favorite Scene

Choose the part of a fairy tale that you liked the best.

Paint or crayon a picture of the scene.

Print a sentence about your picture and paste it on your picture.

....

Creative Activity 6

My Favorite Fairy Tale Character

Choose your favorite fairy tale character.

Using colored paper, scissors, and glue make a picture of the character.

Print a sentence about the character that you chose.

Creative Activity 7

Fairy Tale Puzzle

Choose a scene from your favorite fairy tale.

Draw a picture of the scene.

Color it neatly.

Then cut the scene into puzzle-size pieces.

Give it to a classmate to put together.

Creative Activity 8

Fairy Tale Dinner

Pretend that you are going to cook dinner for a fairy tale character.

Plan a menu.

Write about what you will eat and drink during the meal and what you will have for dessert.

Creative Acitivity 9

Fairy Tale Riddle

Think about the characters in the fairy tales that you have read.

Make up riddles about four different characters.

Example: I am an animal.
           I can bray loudly.
           I helped my friends to find a home.
           I am the _____

Answer Key

Golilocks and the Three Bears

Reading Comprehension:
1. Goldilocks, Papa Bear, Mama Bear, Baby Bear
2. Their porridge was too hot to eat.
3. three bowls of porridge, three chairs, three beds
4. They were just right.
5. Answers will vary.
6. Put a lock on their door.

Phonics:
Pictures to be pasted in the bowl are: box, barn, bat, banana, and ball.

Word Study:
A. 1. soft 2. little 3. warm 4. last 5. on 6. asleep

B. 1. rap 2. small 3. called 4. dishes 5. ate 6. largest 7. sleep 8. forest

The Three Little Pigs

Reading Comprehension:
1. The three little pigs left home.
2. The first pig built a straw house.
3. The stick house was built by the second pig.
4. The third pig built a brick house.
5. The wolf blew in the straw house.
6. The wolf blew in the stick house.
7. The brick house was too strong for the wolf.
8. The wolf slid down the chimney into a pot of hot water.

Phonics:
1. chimney, pigs 2. little, bricks 3. pig, sticks 4. kissed 5. stick, brick 6. big, into 7. quickly, lid 8. lived, happily, brick

Word Study:
1. brick 2. chick 3. thick 4. trick 5. stick 6. pick 7. sick 8. kick

1. chick 2. thick 3. sick 4. trick 5. brick 6. kick 7. pick 8. stick

Little Red Riding Hood

Reading Comprehension:
1. She will stay on the path and not talk to strangers.
2. She stopped to pick flowers and to listen to the birds sing.
3. He knew a shorter way to get to her house.
4. She had big eyes, big ears, and big teeth.
5. The wolf was a villain because he wanted to eat Red Riding Hood.
6. The woodcutter was the hero because he chased the wolf away and saved Red Riding Hood and her Grandmother.

Phonics:
Long a Words: strangers, taking, way, day, same, saved

Short a Words: path, began, grabbed, caps, ran, snack

Word Study:
A. 1. picked, picking
2. jumped, jumping
3. knocked, knocking
4. opened, opening

B. 1. stopped, stopping
2. skipped, skipping
3. grabbed, grabbing

C. 1. lived, living
2. waved, waving
3. smiled, smiling

D. 1. picked 2. lived 3. skipping
4. knocked

The Three Billy Goats Gruff

Reading Comprehension:
1. The troll was the villain because he wouldn't let the goats go across his bridge.
2. Little Billy Goat Gruff and Middle Billy Goat Gruff had to pretend to be brave.
3. Big Billy Goat Gruff was brave and clever.
4. Answers may vary.
5. Answers may vary.
6. Answers may vary.

Phonics:
1. grass 2. bridge 3. troll 4. trip-trap
5. green 6. proudly 7. creak, groan
8. Gruff

Word Study:
A. Answers will vary.
B. 1. big, billy, bridge, butted
2. tiny, trap, trip, troll
3. goats, gobble, grass, gruff
4. saucers, second, straggly, strong
C. 1. large 2. beautiful 3. whispered
4. stopped 5. dark 6. soft 7. under
8. mean 9. little 10. out

The Little Red Hen

Reading Comprehension:
1. The Little Red Hen, the cat, the goose, and the pig were the characters in the story.
2. She found some grains of wheat.
3. She planted the grains and watched them grow.
4. She asked her friends to help her.
5. They would not help her with any of the work.
6. Answers will vary.
7. Answers will vary.

Phonics:
Pictures to be colored are: bell, tent, bed, jet, nest, net, and sled.

Word Study:
A. 1. drake 2. cake 3. snake 4. rake
5. flake 6. shake 7. lake 8. wake

B. 1. flake 2. snake 3. lake 4. rake 5. cake
6. drake 7. wake 8. shake

The Gingerbread Man

Reading Comprehension:
1. She baked a gingerbread man and some cookies.
2. It had raisin eyes and a raisin nose, pink frosting for a mouth, and three cherries for buttons.
3. The gingerbread man jumped out of the oven and ran away.
4. The gingerbread man ran away from the old lady, the old man, the men cutting hay, the horse, and the cow.
5. The fox was very clever.

6. He had the gingerbread man get closer to his mouth and then ate him.

Phonics:

The pictures to be colored blue are: goat, gun, log, goose, gum, and girl.

The pictures to be colored red are: giraffe, cage, giant, gerbil, cottage, and bridge.

Word Study:

A. 1. (2) 2. (3) 3. (2) 4. (2) 5. (3) 6. (1) 7. (3) 8. (1)

B. 1. snowball 2. bedroom 3. beside 4. grandmother 5. afternoon 6. pancake 7. popcorn 8. upstairs

The Ugly Duckling

Reading Comprehension:

1. after 2. during 3. before 4. after 5. after 6. during 7. before 8. during 9. before 10. during

Phonics:

The eggs to be colored contain the following words: bumpy, hungry, rubbed, fluffy, jump, duck, push, turtle.

Word Study:

1. biggest 2. smaller 3. longer 4. shiny 5. cooler 6. ugliest 7. warmer 8. cold

The Elves and the Shoemaker

Reading Comprehension:

1. The shoemaker could not see very well and his fingers worked slowly.
2. Answers will vary.
3. Answers will vary.
4. There was only one piece of leather to make shoes. Answers may also vary.
5. They hid in a dark corner and watched the elves work.
6. They made shoes and clothes for them.

Phonics:

The pictures to be glued onto the shoe are: shell, sheep, shovel, ship, and shark.

Word Study:

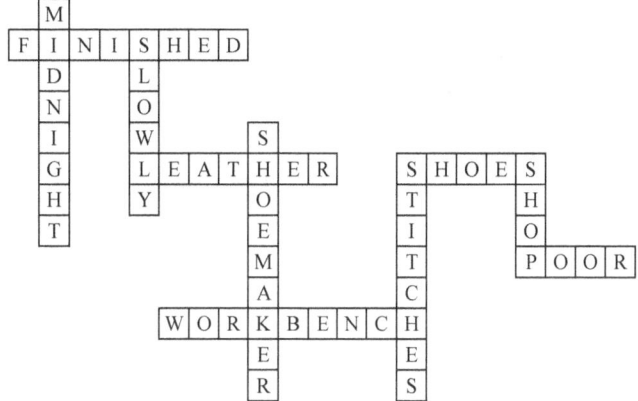

The Four Musicians

Reading Comprehension:

1. The main characters are the donkey, the cat, the dog, and the rooster.
2. Their masters did not want them any more.
3. They were getting too old to do their work.
4. Answers will vary.
5. The donkey kicked and brayed, the cat hissed and scratched, the rooster pecked them, and the dog bit them.
6. They thought a monster had come in their house.

Phonics:
1. sold, old 2. found, hound 3. unkind, blind 4. house, mouse 5. say, today 6. tree, see 7. night, light

Word Study:
Acceptable answers:
1. angry, surprised, worried
2. annoyed, cross, surprised, unhappy
3. excited, happy, pleased, surprised
4. excited, happy, pleased, surprised
5. excited, pleased, happy, surprised
6. frightened, worried, surprised

Jack and the Beanstalk

Reading Comprehension:
Possible answers:

Giant - ugly, man, scary, angry, huge, hungry, grumpy, big, sleepy

Jack - silly, unhappy, small, curious, smart, hungry, boy, kind, young, brave

Giant's Wife - ugly, scary, unhappy, old, woman, angry, kind, big, huge

Jack's Mother - unhappy, woman, angry, kind

Phonics:
1. three bags of gold
2. ugly giant
3. a huge castle
4. a hot bowl of porridge
5. golden egg
6. a singing silver harp
7. a magic hen
8. a big beanstalk

Word Study:
A. 1. morning 2. huge 3. quickly 4. loud 5. shouted 6. after 7. asleep 8. long

B. 1. shouted 2. knock 3. castle 4. silly 5. cottage 6. return 7. grabbed 8. boy

C. without, beanstalk, outside, breakfast, Englishman, into, inside, cupboard

Little Red Riding Hood

 On the way to her Grandmother's house, Red Riding Hood met a wolf.

 The wolf ran to Grandmother's house and locked her in a closet.

 The wolf got in Grandmother's bed and waited for Red Riding Hood.

 Red Riding Hood saw the wolf's big eyes, big ears, and big teeth.

 The wolf jumped out of bed to get Red Riding Hood.

 A woodcutter chased the wolf away with his ax.

Goldilocks and the Three Bears

Goldilocks ate the porridge in Baby Bear's bowl.

Goldilocks broke Baby Bear's chair.

Goldilocks went to sleep in Baby Bear's bed.

The three bears came home.

The three bears looked at their bowls.

The three bears looked at Baby Bear's chair.

The three bears looked at Goldilocks sleeping.

Goldilocks ran away.

The Three Little Pigs

The first little pig built a house of straw.

The wolf huffed and puffed and blew the straw house down.

The second little pig built a house of sticks.

The wolf huffed and puffed and blew the stick house down.

The third little pig built a house made of bricks.

The wolf huffed and puffed but could not blow the brick house down.

So the wolf climbed on the roof and slid down the chimney.

The wolf fell into a pot of boiling water and that was the end of him.

The Elves and the Shoemaker

 The poor shoemaker used his last piece of leather to cut out a pair of shoes.

 The next morning, the shoemaker found a fine pair of shoes on his workbench.

 The shoemaker sold the shoes to a rich man and had enough money to buy leather for two pairs of shoes.

 The next morning the shoemaker found two pairs of perfectly stitched shoes.

 One evening, the shoemaker and his wife decided to hide in a corner of the shop to see who was making the shoes.

 They were surprised when they saw three little elves, without any clothes, busily making shoes.

 The next day the shoemaker and his wife decided to make the elves some shoes and clothes.

 That night they hid in a corner to watch the elves try on their new clothes and then disappear into the night.

Jack and the Beanstalk

 Jack and his mother had to sell the cow for money.

 Jack sold the cow to a man for a bag of magic beans.

 Jack's mother was angry and threw the beans out the window.

 The next morning, there was a big beanstalk outside the house.

 At the top of the beanstalk Jack found a castle and took a bag of gold from the giant.

 The second time Jack took a magic hen that laid golden eggs.

 The third time Jack took a magic harp that could sing.

 Jack chopped down the beanstalk and the giant was killed.

www.ingramcontent.com/pod-product-compliance
Lightning Source LLC
Chambersburg PA
CBHW080438230426
43662CB00015B/2307